Nelson Ph[...]
Spelling and Ha[...]

Pupil Book

Yellow

Anita Warwick   Nicola York
Series Editor: John Jackman

OXFORD
UNIVERSITY PRESS

OXFORD
UNIVERSITY PRESS

Great Clarendon Street, Oxford, OX2 6DP, United Kingdom

Oxford University Press is a department of the University of Oxford.
It furthers the University's objective of excellence in research, scholarship,
and education by publishing worldwide. Oxford is a registered trade mark of
Oxford University Press in the UK and in certain other countries

Text © Anita Warwick and Nicola York 2014
Original illustrations © Oxford University Press 2014

The moral rights of the authors have been asserted

First published by Nelson Thornes Ltd in 2010
This edition published by Oxford University Press in 2014

All rights reserved. No part of this publication may be reproduced,
stored in a retrieval system, or transmitted, in any form or by any
means, without the prior permission in writing of Oxford University
Press, or as expressly permitted by law, by licence or under terms
agreed with the appropriate reprographics rights organization.
Enquiries concerning reproduction outside the scope of the above
should be sent to the Rights Department, Oxford University Press, at
the address above.

You must not circulate this work in any other form and you must
impose this same condition on any acquirer

British Library Cataloguing in Publication Data
Data available

978-1-4085-0605-9

5

Printed in Spain

Acknowledgements

Cover illustration: Alan Rogers
Illustrations: Alan Rogers; Andy Peters; and Mike Philips at Beehive Illustrations
Logo illustration: John Haslam
Page make-up: Wearset Ltd, Boldon, Tyne and Wear

Chief on page 9: Indian chief © Superstock/www.photolibrary.com. **Sky** on page 10: blue sky with cirrus clouds © iStockphoto. **Snow** on page 12: Sierra Nevada mountains, California, USA, 2006 © Simon Weller/Getty Images. **Statue** on page 15: statue in garden © iStockphoto. **Crystal** on page 16: quartz crystal © Mark van Aardt/Getty Images. **Fort** on page 23: © Peter Scholey/www.photolibrary.com. **Floor** on page 23: corridor floor © PhotoStock-Israel/Alamy. **Pearl** on page 24: pearl on oyster shell © WestEnd61/Rex Features. **Snout** on page 26: hedgehog (erinaceus europaeus) juvenile, blonde genetic variation, St Tiggywinkles, Aylesbury, UK © Les Stocker/www.photolibrary.com. **Shear** on page 29: a professional sheep shearer, USA © Getty Images. **Elephant** on page 31: African elephant (loxodonta Africana) and gazelle on savannah © moodboard/Alamy. **School** on page 32: children running holding hands in playground © Bubbles Photolibrary/Alamy. **Pitch** on page 32: aerial view of football pitch in stadium © kolvenbach/Alamy. **Sugar** on page 37: © iStockphoto. **Machine** on page 37: workings inside a watch © iStockphoto. **Circus** on page 38: All Human Circus © Dean Houlding/Rex Features; Hertfordshire County Show, Redbourn, Hertfordshire, 23 May 2009. **Bridge** on page 38: Forth rail bridge across the Firth of Forth, Scotland, © iStockphoto. **Giraffe** on page 38: Rothschild giraffe (giraffa camelopardalis rothschildi) walking, native to Africa © ZSSD/Minden Pictures/FLPA. **Police** on page 39: policewoman crouching to talk to girl (3-5) © Peter Dazeley/Getty Images. **Space** on page 39: galaxy © iStockphoto. **City** on page 40: Glasgow © iStockphoto. **Climb** on page 40: girl climbing rock face at rock climbing school © Strauss/Curtis/www.photolibrary.com. **Stitch** on page 40: satin stitch © Sampson Lloyd/Getty Images. **Weather** on page 41: John Kettley © Andrew Drysdale/Rex Features. **Happy** on page 50: smiling creative girl © iStockphoto. **Lipstick** on page 55: © zuing/ Fotolia.com. **Fingerprint** on page 55: © iStockphoto. **pour** on page 56: pouring milk © AAGAMIA/ Getty Images. **Hare** on page 56: European hare (lepus europaeus) adult, running, Cley Marshes, Norfolk Wildlife Trust Reserve, Cley-next-the Sea, Norfolk, England © Roger Tidman/FLPA. **Geese** on page 60: © Dan Burn-Forti/Getty Images. **Pride** on page 61: pride of lions © iStockphoto.

Although we have made every effort to trace and contact all
copyright holders before publication this has not been possible in all
cases. If notified, the publisher will rectify any errors or omissions at
the earliest opportunity.

Links to third party websites are provided by Oxford in good faith
and for information only. Oxford disclaims any responsibility for
the materials contained in any third party website referenced in
this work.

Contents

UNIT			PAGE
Yellow	1	Modifier **e**	4
Yellow	2	Alternative spellings **ai** phoneme	6
Yellow	3	Alternative spellings **ee** phoneme	8
Yellow	4	Alternative spellings **igh** phoneme	10
Yellow	5	Alternative spellings **oa** phoneme	12
Yellow	6	Alternative spellings **oo** phoneme	14
Yellow	7	Alternative spellings for **e, i, o**	16
Yellow	8	Alternative spellings review	18
Yellow	9	Alternative spellings **zh** phoneme	20
Yellow	10	Alternative spellings **or** phoneme	22
Yellow	11	Alternative spellings **ur** phoneme	24
Yellow	12	Alternative spellings **ow, oi** phonemes	26
Yellow	13	Alternative spellings **ear, air** phonemes	28
Yellow	14	Alternative spellings review	30
Yellow	15	Alternative spellings **c** and **ch**	32
Yellow	16	Silent letters	34
Yellow	17	Alternative spellings **sh**	36
Yellow	18	Soft **c** and soft **g**	38
Yellow	19	Alternative spellings review	40
Yellow	20	Punctuation	42
Yellow	21	Word endings **ed**	44
Yellow	22	Word endings **s**	46
Yellow	23	Word endings **ing**	48
Yellow	24	Word endings **er** and **est**	50
Yellow	25	Word endings **ly**	52
Yellow	26	Compound words	54
Yellow	27	Homophones	56
Yellow	28	Irregular past tense	58
Yellow	29	Irregular plurals	60
Yellow	30	Review spelling rules	62

How to use this book — 64

Yellow 1

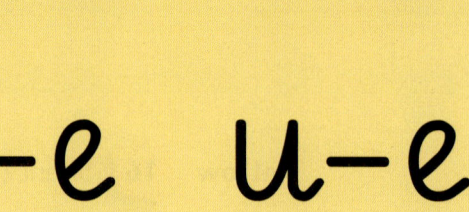

a-e i-e
o-e u-e

I would like to ride a bike.

Focus A

Copy the letter patterns into your book.

ate ate ate ate ate   ote ote ote ote ote

ite ite ite ite ite ite   ute ute ute ute ute

Focus B

Word bank

bake   tape
cake   cane
plate   mane
bike   ride
bite   ripe
kite   shine
pipe   write
bone   hope
code   vote
cube   tune
flute   salute
tube
to   into

Add **e** to these words and write the new words.

1. can + e
2. tap + e 
3. cub + e 
4. tub + e 
5. pip + e 
6. kit + e 

TIP If you add an **e** to the end of a word, it changes the middle vowel sound to a long sound:
pin → pine   hop → hope   rip → ripe.

4 Yellow 1: To learn how the addition of an 'e' affects the vowel sound.

Extra

Choose **ate**, **ite**, **ote** or **ute** to complete these words. Copy the words into your book.

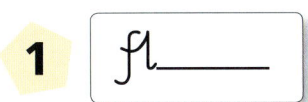

1. fl____
2. v____
3. sal____
4. b____   
5. pl____
6. wr____

Extension

Copy and complete each sentence using words from the box.

You can hum a ____.

A dog can eat a ____.

A light will ____ at night.

I want to ____ a ____.

bone
bake
tune
shine
cake

Yellow 2

ai

They wanted to play, but it started to rain!

Focus A

Copy the letters into your book.

ai ai ai ai ai   ey ey ey ey ey

ay ay ay ay ay ay

TIP ay comes at the end of words: b**ay** st**ay** pl**ay**.
ai comes at the beginning or middle of words: w**ai**t m**ai**n **ai**m.

Focus B

sat

word bank

aim   stain
afraid train
main   wait
paint grain
faint main

bay   tray
play   sway
spray stay

acorn grey
cake   straight
eight great
no   go

Use the tip to help you complete the words. Copy the words into your book.

1 p___nt
2 tr___ 
3 afr___d 
4 spr___ 
5 st___n 
6 pl___ 

TIP Remember the magic e that can make an ai sound as well, as in c**a**ke and sn**a**ke.

6 Yellow 2: To learn alternative spellings for /ai/.

Extra

Find the hidden **ay** or **ai** words in the boxes below.
Write the words in your book.

1. hy**train**kiso
2. dt**grain**okp
3. rts**way**dhy
4. mdu**faint**jkl
5. gy**spray**jucl
6. **main**tilpgr

Extension

There are other ways to spell the **ai** sound.
Copy the words below into your book.
Underline the letters which make the **ai** sound.

1. eight
2. straight 
3. great 
4. cake 
5. grey 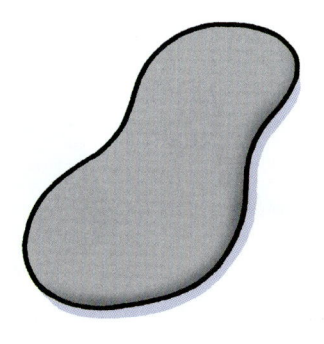
6. acorn

Yellow 3

ee

I am very happy when I see the sea!

Focus A

Copy the letter patterns into your book.

ee ee ee ee ee   ea ea ea ea ea ea

y y y y y   ei ei ei ei ei ei

Focus B

Word bank

beat   mean
dream   sea
meat   tea
tree   sleep
see   feet
daddy   jolly
happy   mummy
jelly
ceiling chief
shield
honey   monkey
he   we

Copy and complete the words.

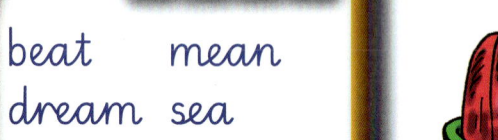

1. jell__
2. tr__ 
3. dr__m 
4. m__t 
5. dadd__ 
6. f__t 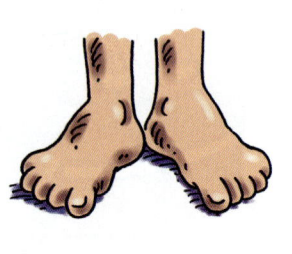

TIP Which spelling? Say the word and clap the number of syllables. If it has one, use **ee** or **ea**. If it has two or more, use **y**.

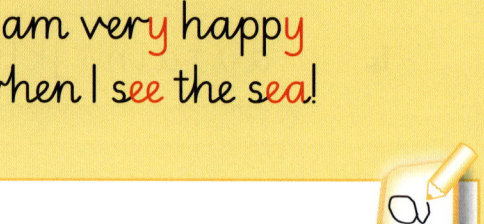

Yellow 3: To learn alternative spellings for /ee/.

Extra

Read the words and write the one that does not rhyme.

1. sweet | beat | sleep | street | meat | greet
2. tree | sea | free | tea | see | feet
3. jolly | dolly | lolly | jelly | holly | brolly
4. mean | dream | steam | team | cream | seem

Extension

Copy the words and underline the letters which make the **ee** sound.

1. monkey
2. honey 
3. he 
4. ceiling 
5. chief 
6. shield

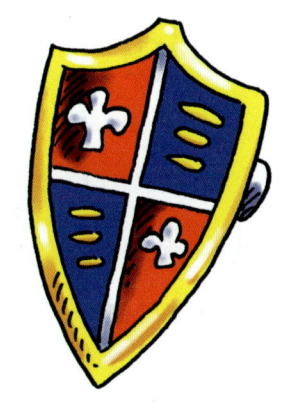

Yellow 4

igh

I tried to fly, but I didn't get very high!

Focus A

Copy the letter patterns into your book.

igh igh igh igh igh   i   i   i   i   i

ie ie ie ie ie ie

TIP igh is often followed by t: night sight.

Focus B

word bank

cried tie
die   tied
pie
cry   shy
dry   sky
fly   try
fright sight
light night
child mind
find   wild
kind
like

Copy and complete the words.

1 ch__ld
2 p__ 
3 cr__d 
4 fr__t 
5 t__ 
6 sk__ 

TIP Remember the **igh** sound can be made by a modifier **e**:   bite bike.

10   Yellow 4: To learn alternative spellings for /igh/.

Extra

Choose an **igh**, **y**, **ie** or **i** word to describe each picture.

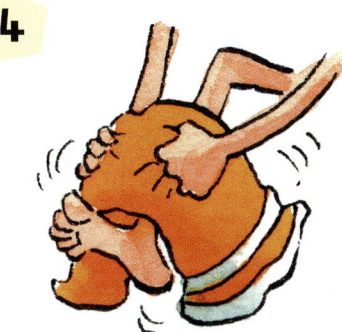

1. 2. 3.
4. 5. 6.

| fly | light | tied | night | dry | kind |

Extension

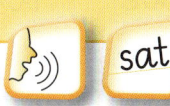

Copy and complete these sentences using an **igh** word.

A baby will often ____.

A loud bang gave me a ____.

The wind on the hill was ____.

The new ____ was ____.

fright
child
shy
cry
wild

11

Yellow 5

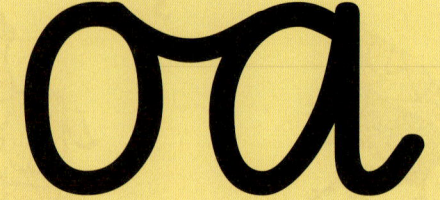

oa

The sn**ow** on the r**oa**d means the car g**oe**s sl**ow**ly.

Focus A

Copy the letter patterns into your book.

oa oa oa oa oa   oe oe oe oe oe

ow ow ow ow ow

Focus B

TIP
oa comes in the middle of a word: t**oa**d fl**oa**t m**oa**n.
ow normally comes at the end of a short or long word: b**ow** mell**ow** sh**ow**.
oe often comes at the end of a short word: J**oe** d**oe** g**oe**s.
o can come in the middle or at the end of a word: n**o** g**o** s**o** b**o**th.

sat

word bank

doe   toe
goes
bow   snow
bowl   mellow
show   shadow
boat   road
float   toad
moan   cloak
both   ghost
hero
so   oh

Use the tip to help you write the complete words in your book.

1 her__
2 shad__
3 cl__k
4 b__t
5 t__
6 sn__

TIP Remember the magic **e** that can make an **oa** sound as well, as in b**o**n**e** and sm**o**k**e**.

12 Yellow 5: To learn alternative spellings for /oa/.

Extra

Write two words which rhyme with each of the words below.

1 snow
2 road 
3 moan 
4 toast 
5 toes 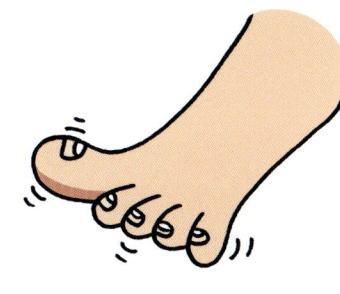
6 bowl 

Extension

Copy the sentences into your book.
Draw a picture to illustrate each one.

1 A toad in a coat is on the telephone!
2 A goat is in the snow, holding a rose.
3 A ghost is eating toast on a pillow.
4 A boat is driving on a road!

Yellow 6

oo

You should see the blue goose in the zoo!

Focus A

Copy the letter patterns into your book.

oo oo oo oo oo   ew ew ew ew ew

ue ue ue ue ue   ou ou ou ou ou

Focus B

TIP
oo often comes in the middle of words: b**oo**t sp**oo**n f**oo**d.
ue often comes at the end of short and long words: c**ue** arg**ue** tr**ue**.
ew often comes at the end of short words: bl**ew** fl**ew** kn**ew**.
ou is often followed by **ld**: w**ou**ld c**ou**ld sh**ou**ld.

word bank

zoo   spoon
boot   goose
food   moose
moon
cue   glue
true   argue
blue   tissue
statue
blew   chew
flew   stew
knew   screw
threw
cute
could   should
would
do

Use the tip to help you write the complete words in your book.

1 m___se
2 gl___
3 tiss___
4 bl___
5 ch___
6 st___

TIP Remember the modifier **e** can make an **oo** sound as well, as in t**u**n**e** and fl**u**t**e**.

Yellow 6: To learn alternative spellings for /oo/.

Extra

Write the correct spelling of each word in your book.

1. moon | muen
2. scroo | screw 
3. statew | statue 
4. cewt | cute 
5. spoon | spune 
6. throo | threw 

Extension

Find as many **oo**-sounding words as you can in the word search.

b	l	u	e		q			t			v
l	v	w	d	s	o	o	n	h	c	h	e	w
e	n	t	o		p	z	t		r	g	l	
w	g	l	u	e		v	s	u	e	o		g
	b	l	o	o	m		p		w	o	n	t	y
			r		o	a	o		w	s	e		o
a	r	g	u	e	o		o	v		e	w	l	p
c	u	e	z		n		n	d	d	v		f	x

Record the words that you have found in a grid like this:

oo	ue	ew
	blue	

15

Yellow 7

e i
o

Ready Steady Teddy
History Mystery! The Top Wasp Squad

Focus A

Practise the horizontal join from **w** to **a**.

wa wa wa wa wa

wha wha wha wha

TIP
In the middle of words the **e** sound can be written as **ea**: head ready.
i (pin) can be written as **y**: gym mystery.
o (box) can be **a** after **w** or **qu**: was squash.

Focus B

word bank

head   instead
bread   breakfast
feather weather
thread dead
spread ready

gym   mystery
crystal pyramid

was   watch
want   wasp
squad   squash
squat
what

Write the complete words in your book.

1 p_ramid    2 w_tch    3 br___d

4 cr_stal    5 f___ther    6 squ__t

Yellow 7: To learn alternative spellings for /e/, /i/ and /o/.

Extra

Blend the phonemes to make complete words. Write each word in your book.

1. i + n + s + t + ea + d =
2. m + y + s + t + er + y =
3. s + qu + a + sh =
4. w + ea + th + er =

Extension

All of these words use the **ea** spelling pattern to make an **e** sound. Unscramble the letters, then write the words in your book.

1.  d e h a
2.  f t k b r a a s e
3.  t d r e h a
4.  s d e r a p
5.  a d d e

Yellow 8

Can you remember all the spelling patterns?

TIP Remember: not all words follow the usual spelling pattern! Use the word banks from earlier pages to help you.

Focus

sat

Find and write eight pairs of rhyming words.
Think of three more words to rhyme with each pair.

spite

toe

treat

eight

mystery

tissue

bread

squat

zoo

shadow

history

plate

meet

bed

hot

fright

18 Yellow 8: To review alternative spellings for phonemes.

Extra

Identify the sounds for each creepy-crawly word.
Choose letters from the box to write each word.

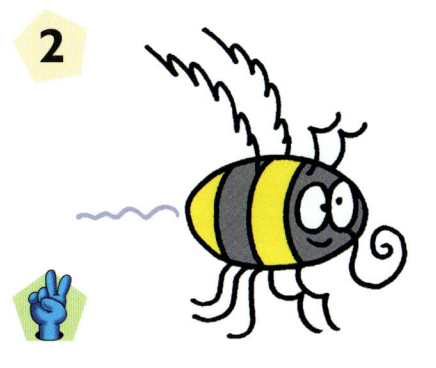

1.
2.
3.
4.
5.

vowel sounds:
a ai ee er i y

consonant sounds:
b d f l n p s w

Extension

Copy and complete the sentences using words from the box.

An ____ is a joint in your arm.

I ____ in my warm cosy bed.

I got in a ____ to fly to Spain.

My shoes are too ____.

My nan likes to ____ her roses.

plane
prune
sleep
tight
elbow

Yellow 9

zh

The measure of treasure is the pleasure it gives.

Focus A

Copy the letter patterns into your book.

si si si si si   su su su su su

TIP The **zh** sound is normally written as an **s**: lei**s**ure plea**s**ure ca**s**ual.
It can be written as: vi**si**on bei**ge** gara**ge**.

Focus B

Use the tip to help you write the complete words in your book.

word bank

leisure
measure
pleasure
treasure
usual
casual
unusual

vision
decision
division
version
television

beige
garage
she

1 televi___on    2 gara___    3 trea___ure

4 bei___    5 mea___ure    6 divi___on

Yellow 9: To recognise, say and write the /zh/ phoneme.

Extra

Make two lists of words that contain the spelling patterns **sure** and **sion**.

sure   sion

Extension

Choose two **zh** words from the word bank to help you copy and complete the sentence.

What an _____ way to _____ your feet!

Yellow 10

or

Four kittens patted a ball with their paws.

Focus A

Copy the letter patterns into your book.

al al al al al   aw aw aw aw aw

TIP
or can be anywhere in a word: **or**der p**or**t f**or**.
our often comes at the end of words: f**our** p**our** y**our**.
al often comes before l or k: b**all** sm**all** t**al**k.
aw usually comes at the end of short words: p**aw** j**aw** cl**aw**.

Focus B

word bank

for / order
port / orbit
four / your
pour / court
ball / small
wall / talk
walk
paw / draw
jaw / yawn
saw / claw
caught / poor
taught / pause
shore / floor
called

Use the spelling tips to write the complete words in your book.

1 ___bit
2 f___ 
3 w___l  
4 s___ 
5 w___k 
6 cl___ 

22   Yellow 10: To learn alternative spellings for /or/.

Extra

Write the correct spelling of each word in your book.

1. fort / fourt
2. por / paw 
3. ball / bawl 
4. dror / draw 
5. yawn / yourn 
6. calt / court 

Extension

There are more ways to spell the **or** sound. Copy the words below, and underline the letters which make the **or** sound.

1. caught
2. poor 
3. shore 
4. pause 
5. taught 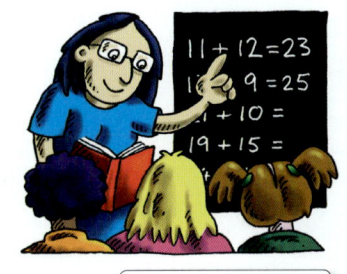
6. floor

Yellow 11

ur

The **ea**rly b**ir**d catches the w**or**m.

Focus A

Practise the horizontal joins from **o** to **r** and **i** to **r**.

or or or or or   ir ir ir ir ir ir

TIP
ur normally comes in the middle or end of words: b**ur**n f**ur** sp**ur**.
ir normally comes in the middle of short words: f**ir**st b**ir**th b**ir**d.
ear normally comes at the start or middle of words: **ear**ly **ear**n p**ear**l.
or normally comes after a **w**: w**or**d w**or**k w**or**th.

Focus B

word bank
fur
spur
bird
birth
first
earn
early
pearl
word
work
little
turtle
burn
skirt
girl
shirt
earth
search
worm
worth

sat

Use the tip to help you write the complete words in your book.

1 w___m
2 b___n 
3 ___th 
4 sk___t 
5 p___l 
6 g___l 

24 Yellow 11: To learn alternative spellings for /ur/.

Extra

Find the hidden **ur**, **ir**, **ear** or **or** words in the boxes below.
Write them in your book.

1. yhturtlejulz
2. gipmxearly
3. qumiworkl
4. shuishirtolr
5. searchuygd
6. bbirthkilmn

Extension

Find as many **ur** words as you can in the word search.

	w	s	i	r	c	h	u	r	c	h		l
	f	s	s	f	i	r	s	t	t	b	l	e
q	u	k	p	u			w	p	u	u		a
	r	i	u	r	a	c	o	e	r	r		b	r
p	u	r	r	r	q		r	a	t	n		i	n
		t	b	y		b	k	r	l		s	r
	z		t		g	i	r	l	e	k		d
h	e	a	r	d					p	u	r	s	e

Record the words that you have found in a grid like this:

ur	ir	ear
	skirt	

Yellow 12

ow
oi

There's a mouse in the house!
Oh, it's just a toy, you naughty boy.

Focus A

Copy the letter patterns into your book.

oy oy oy oy oy
ou ou ou ou ou

TIP: ow (as in how) can be written as ou in the middle of words: loud sound scout.
oi (as in join) should always be written as oy at the ends of words: joy annoy enjoy.

Focus B

Use the tip to help you write the complete words in your book.

Word bank
- loud
- sound
- cloud
- scout
- snout
- house
- boy
- joy
- toy
- annoy
- cowboy
- could
- down
- cow
- now
- shout
- out
- mouse
- point
- soil
- join
- enjoy

1. t___
2. cl___d 
3. cowb___ 
4. sn___t 
5. enj___ 
6. h___se 

Yellow 12: To learn alternative spellings for /ow/ and /oi/.

Extra

Solve these riddles – the answers are all **oy** or **oi** words.

1. Children like to play with one of these.
2. You dig in this to plant seeds in your garden.
3. You do this to show a direction.
4. If you are not a girl, you are one of these.
5. You do this when you put two things together.

Extension

Copy and complete the poem, choosing an **ow** or **ou** word from the box.

mouse   house   cow   down   out   shout   now

Clara the ____ had a very neat ____
But then one day she saw a ____.
She chased it up and ____ the stair
But ____ the ____ was in her hair.
Clara sat ____ and began to ____
"I don't want you here. Get ____! Get ____!"

Yellow 13

ear
air

Here is a deer!
Where?
There, near the bear.

Focus A

Copy the letter patterns into your book.

eer   eer eer eer eer   are   are are are are

ere   ere ere ere ere

Focus B

TIP The sounds **ear** and **air** are often spelt differently at the ends of words. Here are some examples:
ear – h**ere** ch**eer**.
air – c**are** p**ear** now**here**.
Some of the spellings have other sounds, so try not to get confused.

word bank

here   severe
interfere
deer   cheer
peer
care   share
square
pear   bear
tear
there   where
nowhere
their

Choose the correct letters to complete these words.

1 sev____    2 d____    3 ch____

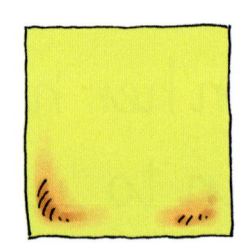

4 squ____    5 p____    6 wh____

28   Yellow 13: To learn alternative spellings for /ear/ and /air/.

Extra

All of these words contain the **ear** spelling pattern, but they have different sounds. Complete the words.

1. b____
2. t____ 
3. h____t 
4. l____n 
5. w____ 
6. sh____ 

Extension

What does it mean? Write the meaning of each of these words in your book. An example has been done for you.

repair: mend something that is broken

1. scare
2. pair
3. clear
4. appear
5. share

Yellow 14

Can you remember all of the spelling patterns?

TIP Remember: not all words follow the usual spelling pattern! Use a dictionary if you need to.

Focus A

Look at the possible spellings underneath each picture. Copy the correct spelling for each word.

1. talk / tork
2. world / wirld 
3. mowse / mouse 
4. boi / boy 
5. deer / dere 
6. bair / bear 

Yellow 14: To review alternative spellings for phonemes.

Extra

Find a smaller word in each of these longer words.

TIP Finding small words inside bigger words can help you learn to spell them: I put ice in my juice.

1 computer
2 tomorrow 
3 donkey 
4 elephant 
5 island 
6 rainbow 

Extension

Now have a go at hiding these smaller words in bigger words! An example has been done for you.

ring   earring   spring

1 out
2 late
3 age
4 hen
5 key

Yellow 15

c
ch

School is cool,
you can play catch and chase.

Focus A

Copy the letter patterns into your book.

ch ch ch ch ch   tch tch tch tch tch

TIP
c is sometimes written as **ch**: **ch**ord **ch**orus a**ch**e.
ch is often written as **tch**
at the end of words: ca**tch** fe**tch** sti**tch**.
sometimes it is just a **t**
when followed by **ure**: fu**t**ure na**t**ure.

Focus B

word bank

chord
chorus
choir
ache
school

future
nature
picture
denture

catch
fetch
stitch
pitch
match

asked

Write the complete words in your book.

1 s___ool    2 pic___ure    3 ma___

4 den___ure    5 pi___    6 ___oir

Yellow 15: To learn alternative spellings for /c/ and /ch/.

Extra

Read the words in each box. Copy the word which does not rhyme.

1. stitch   witch   pitch   catch   ditch

2. catch   match   snatch   patch   fetch

3. watch   fetch   stretch   sketch   etch

4. hutch   blush   much   touch   clutch

Extension

Find the answers to these questions using words from the box.

1. You can paint or draw one of these.

2. You go here to learn.

3. You might go and see a football one.

4. If you run a long way, your legs might do this.

5. If you throw a ball, you might then do this.

match   ache   picture   school   catch

Yellow 16

mb gn
kn wr

The lamb knows how to knit the gnat a hat.

TIP Some common letter patterns contain silent letters. Which letter is the silent one?
mb as in cli**mb**   gn as in **gn**at
kn as in **kn**ow   **wr** as in **wr**ap

Focus A

Copy the letter patterns into your book.

mb mb mb mb mb   gn gn gn gn gn
kn kn kn kn kn   wr wr wr wr wr

Focus B

word bank

climb
lamb
thumb

gnat
sign

know
knife
knit
knot

wrap
write
when

Can you finish these words by using a silent letter grapheme?

1 si___

2 thu___

3 ___ife

4 la___

5 ___ot

6 ___ite

Yellow 16: To learn the silent letters.

Extra

Write these words in alphabetical order.

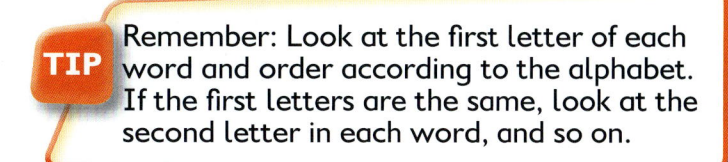

TIP Remember: Look at the first letter of each word and order according to the alphabet. If the first letters are the same, look at the second letter in each word, and so on.

1. lamb comb bomb
2. sign design gnat
3. wrap write wrong

Extension

Copy these words in alphabetical order into your book. Underline the letters that you cannot hear.

autumn    wrap    hour

gnome    badge    biscuit

Yellow 17

sh

*Atten**tion**! Musi**ci**an's spe**ci**al offer!*

Focus A

Copy the letter patterns into your book.

tion   **cian**

sion   **cial**

Focus B

TIP The **sh** sound is very common — and often hidden! With these words, you can hear the **ti**on or **ci**al sound, but there is no **sh** in sight!
cap**tion**   pa**ssion**   opti**cian**   spe**cial**

word bank

attention
caption
station
mention
passion
session
optician
musician
magician
special
facial
social
should

Blend the two parts of the word together. Write the new word in your book. Underline the letters that make the **sh** sound.

1. sta + tion =
2. ses + sion =
3. magi + cian =
4. fa + cial =
5. so + cial =
6. men + tion =

36   Yellow 17: To learn alternative spellings for /sh/.

Extra

Here are other words that contain a **sh** sound. Copy the words, and underline the letters which make the **sh** sound.

1. sugar
2. patient 
3. ocean 
4. machine 
5. chef 
6. tissue 

Extension

Find as many **tion** and **sion** words as you can in the word search.

m	i	s	s	i	o	n	p	a	s	s	i	o	n
s	s	f		t				k		v			p
t	b	e		a	d	d	i	t	i	o	n		t
a		s		c			d	g			n	t	
t		s	f	t		m	a	n	s	i	o	n	
i	s	i		i	q			p			l		z
o		o	l	o			r		s				w
n		n		n		m	e	n	t	i	o	n	

Record the words that you have found in a grid like this:

tion	sion

37

Yellow 18

Soft c
Soft g

Cycle over the bridge.

Focus A

Copy the letter patterns into your book.

ge ge ge ge ge ge   ice ice ice ice ice

dge dge dge dge dge

Focus B

TIP Sometimes the hard sounds **c** and **g** can be big softies.
s is often **c** before an i, e or y: **c**ity i**c**e **c**ycle.
j is often **g** if it comes before a vowel: **g**entle lar**g**e.
often at the end of the word, you use **dge**: ri**dge** le**dge**.

word bank

city   rice
ice   police
cycle   space
circus   circle

gentle   giraffe
general   angel

ridge   judge
ledge   orange
hedge   bridge

come   one

Choose the correct letters to complete these words.

1 ___ircus

2 an___el

3 bri___

4 ___iraffe

5 ju___

6 ri___e

38   Yellow 18: To learn alternative spellings for /s/ and /j/.

Extra

Blend the phonemes to make complete words. Write each word in your book, then draw a picture of it.

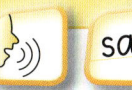

1. c + ir + c + le =
2. h + e + dge =
3. d + a + n + g + er =
4. c + y + c + le =

Extension

All of these words use a soft **c** or **g**. Unscramble the letters and write the words in your book.

1. ugglaeg
2. ognaer
3. ttocgea
4. olicpe
5. cesap

Yellow 19

Can you remember all the spelling patterns?

TIP There are some letters that can make different sounds, as well as sounds which are spelled in different ways. Give it a go, then check. Remember you can always check in a dictionary.

Focus

Look at the possible spellings underneath each picture. Copy the correct spelling for each word.

1. city / sity
2. climb / clim 
3. shugar / sugar 
4. stitch / stich 
5. larj / large 
6. write / rite 

Yellow 19: To learn alternative spellings for phonemes.

Extra

TIP You can use silly sentences to help you remember how to spell tricky words. 'Big elephants can't always use small exits' helps to spell 'because'.

Read these sentences, then write the word they help to spell.

1. People eat orange peel like emus.

2. Dogs only eat sausages!

3. Sally Anne is dancing.

4. Rhythm has your two hips moving!

Extension

Write your own silly sentences to help you remember how to spell these words.

1. weather

2. beauty

3. danger

4. castle

5. sudden

Yellow 20 Punctuation

"You can do it!" "No, I can't"

Focus A

Copy the punctuation marks into your book.

' ,
! .

Focus B

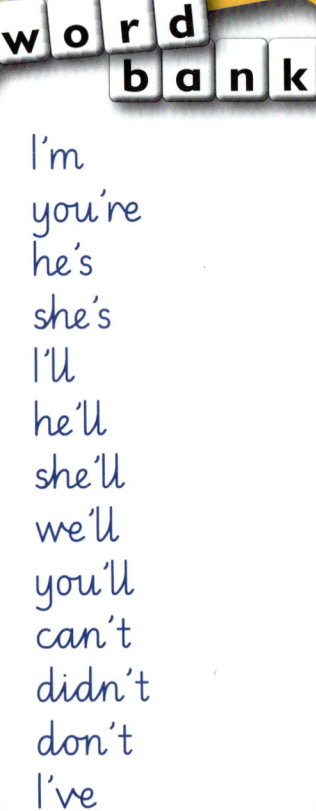

word bank

I'm
you're
he's
she's
I'll
he'll
she'll
we'll
you'll
can't
didn't
don't
I've
Mr
Mrs

TIP When contracting words, you remove some letters, squash the others together, then add the apostrophe where the missing letters are!

Turn these words into contracted words.

1. I am
2. he is
3. she will
4. we will
5. can not
6. do not

Turn these contracted words into long words.

1. you're
2. she's
3. I'll
4. he'll
5. won't
6. didn't

42 Yellow 20: To learn the spelling of contracted words. To practise the use of punctuation.

Extra

Read these sentences. Write which sentence type they are.

1 I've got a new puppy!

2 Can you come round to play?

3 Go and get a cloth to clean this up.

4 The party is on Friday.

TIP There are different types of sentence that you can use in your writing.
A question asks something and uses a question mark: ?
An exclamation says something exciting and uses an exclamation mark: !
A statement gives information and uses a full stop: .
A command tells you to do something and uses a full stop too: .

Extension

Copy these sentences, and put either !, ? or . at the end.

1 My favourite colour is yellow

2 Don't you want any more

3 Put your pencils away

4 I'm going on holiday

5 Do you think he'll mind

43

Yellow 21

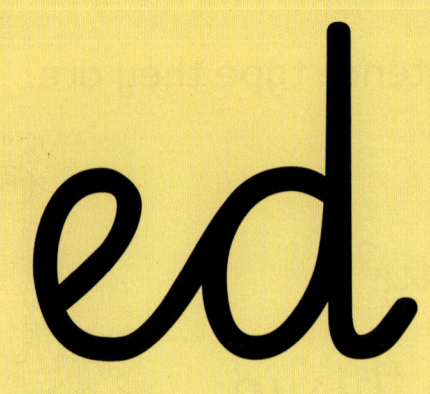

ed

I hopp**ed**, skipp**ed** and jump**ed** as I hurri**ed** home.

Focus A

Copy the letter patterns into your book.

ed   ced
ied   ked

Focus B

TIP: Any word which is a doing word is called a verb. When the action has been done, we use the verb in a 'past tense'. To do this, most words add **ed** without any other changes: play → play**ed**. Words which end in **e** take off **e** and add **ed**: amaze → amaz**ed**.

sat

word bank

cooked
played
jumped
washed
danced
balanced
amazed
typed
batted
hopped
skipped
hurried
carried
cried
looked

Add **ed** to these words. Write the words in your book.

1. jump
2. wash 
3. type 
4. dance 
5. balance 
6. cook 

44 Yellow 21: To add '–ed' to the end of a word; to join other letters to the letter 'd'.

Extra

TIP When a word has a short vowel sound followed by a single consonant, double the consonant before adding **ed**. For example: dro**p** + ed = dro**pp**ed.

Copy the four words below which contain a short vowel sound. Turn the words into the past tense and write each one in a sentence.

| pop | bat | smile | tap | skip |

Extension

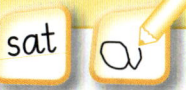

Use the pictures to complete the sentences.

TIP If a noun ends in a **y** you need to change the **y** to an **i** before adding **ed**: **try → tried**.
But, if the letter before the **y** is a vowel, you only need to add **ed**: **enjoy → enjoyed**.

Yesterday, Hassan _____ _____.

Yesterday, Tom _____ _____.

Yesterday, Chen _____ _____ heavy _____.

Yellow 22

Plurals

s
es

There were lots of bear**s**, fox**es** and pon**ies** at the zoo.

TIP Remember: join to the top of the letter **s** and bring your pencil back round.

Focus A

Copy the letter patterns into your book.

es es es es es es   ees ees ees ees ees

ies ies ies ies ies   hes hes hes hes

Focus B

TIP One of something is called a singular noun. Two or more becomes a plural noun: one pot → two pots. You usually add **s** to the singular noun to make the plural.

Write the plural for each of these nouns.

word bank
cats   books
bears   trees
tables pens
windows
foxes
glasses
matches
churches
ponies
pennies
ladies
babies
they

1 cat
2 tree 
3 table 
4 book 
5 window 
6 pen 

46   Yellow 22: To make plurals: to join to the letter 's'.

Extra

TIP If a noun ends in a buzzing sound (sh, ch, ss, x, zz), usually you add **es**: match → match**es**.

Copy and complete these words, putting them in the plural.

1 church___
2 box___
3 kiss___
4 torch___   
5 brush___
6 glass___

Extension

Copy and complete these sentences by adding the plural.

1 One baby, lots of _____.
2 One penny, lots of _____.
3 One toy, lots of _____.
4 One story, lots of _____.
5 One boy, lots of _____.

TIP If a noun ends in a **y**, you usually need to change the **y** to an **i** before adding **es**: lady → ladies.
But, if the letter before the **y** is a vowel, you only need to add **s**:
ray → rays.

47

Yellow 23

TIP Remember: when joining a small letter, the join usually goes to the top of the next letter.

ing

The k**ing** is sing**ing**.

Focus A

Copy the letter patterns into your book.

| ing ing ing ing ing | hing hing hing hing |
| ning ning ning ning | king king king king |

Focus B

TIP Most words add **ing** without any changes:
walk → walk**ing**.
Words which end in an **e**, take off the **e**, then add **ing**:
close → clos**ing**.
Double the final letter if the word has a short vowel sound:
ch**a**t → cha**tt**ing.

word bank
- walking
- talking
- washing
- cooking
- looking
- closing
- typing
- shaking
- making
- chatting
- clapping
- running
- coming

Add an **ing** to these words. Write the new words in your book.

1. clap
2. wash 
3. shake 
4. type 
5. run 
6. cook 

48 Yellow 23: To add '–ing' to the end of a word; to join letters using a diagonal join.

Extra

Copy the sentences using the correct verb.

1. Yesterday I [played] [playing] with my friends.
2. Today I am [played] [playing] with my friends.

3. Yesterday we [jumping] [jumped] in the pool.
4. Today we are [jumping] [jumped] in the pool.

5. Yesterday I [finished] [finishing] all my work.
6. Today I am [finished] [finishing] all my work.

7. Yesterday I [walking] [walked] the dog.
8. Today I am [walking] [walked] the dog.

Extension

Complete the sentences to describe the pictures.

1.
2.
3.

Mary is ____. Lucia is ____. Lucas is ____.

Yellow 24: er est

TIP: When making comparing words most words add **er** or **est**:
 tall → tall**er** → tall**est**.
Words ending with **e**, drop the **e**:
 close → clos**er** → clos**est**.
Double the final letter when a word has a short vowel:
 thin → thin**ner** → thin**nest**.
With words ending with **y,** change the **y** to an **i**:
 craz**y** → craz**ier** → craz**iest**.

tall taller tallest

Focus A

Copy the letter patterns into your book.

er er er er er er er   est est est est est
ier ier ier ier ier ier   iest iest iest iest

Focus B

sat

Add **er** and **est** to these words. Write the new words in your book.

word bank

taller / tallest
quicker / quickest
smaller / smallest

closer / closest
later / latest

thinner / thinnest
hotter / hottest

crazier / craziest
happier / happiest
scarier / scariest

were

1 happy
2 quick 
3 hot 
4 late 
5 scary 
6 small 

50 Yellow 24: To add '–er' and '–est' to the end of a word; to join letters using a diagonal join.

Extra

TIP When you add **er** and **est** to an adjective, you are comparing them.
She is tall, but he is tall**er**.
When you compare more than two things, add **est**.
The dog was big, the cow was big**ger**, but the horse was big**gest**.

Complete these sentences.

The rabbit is small. The rat is _____.
The mouse is _____.

Baby Bear's porridge was hot. Mummy Bear's porridge was _____. Daddy Bear's porridge was _____.

The bear was hairy, the man was _____, and the gorilla was _____.

Extension

Write your own sentences using these adjectives.

1. bright, brighter, brightest
2. pretty, prettier, prettiest
3. hot, hotter, hottest

Yellow 25

ly

He happ**ily** walked quick**ly** down the stairs.

Focus A

Copy the letter patterns into your book.

ily ily ily ily ily ily   kly kly kly kly kly kly

ely ely ely ely ely ely   tly tly tly tly tly tly

Focus B

TIP: For most words, add **ly** without any changes: quick → quick**ly**.
For words ending in **y**, change **y** to an **i**: happy → happ**ily**.

Add **ly** to these words. Write the new words in your book.

word bank

quickly
quietly
slowly
loudly
bravely
sadly

merrily
cheerily
heavily
angrily
luckily
happily
creepily

my

1. heavy
2. slow 
3. angry 
4. loud 
5. lucky 
6. brave 

52   Yellow 25: To add '–ly' to the end of a word; to join to an ascender.

Extra

Copy and complete these sentences, changing the adjective to an adverb.

| slow | Tom walked _____ through the house. |

| heavy | The rain fell _____ from the sky. |

| quiet | The mouse scampered _____ past the cat. |

| quick | Rose won the race because she ran _____. |

| happy | _____, Kim hugged her new puppy. |

Extension

Write your own sentences using these adverbs.

1. loudly
2. sadly
3. merrily
4. creepily

Yellow 26

Compound words

At playtime we play football on the playground.

Focus A

TIP Remember to join letters carefully, making sure they are evenly spaced.

Copy the letter patterns into your book.

oot oot oot oot oot   oon oon oon oon
ool ool ool ool ool   oom oom oom oom

Focus B

TIP A compound word is two words that have been put together to make a new word.

word bank
- playtime
- playground
- football
- baseball
- paintball
- paintbrush
- toolbox
- paintbox
- grandfather
- grandmother
- airport
- ferryport
- some

Copy and finish these word sums, to make compound words.

1. paint + brush =
2. tool + box =
3. grand + father =
4. air + port =
5. bath + room =
6. cow + boy =

54 Yellow 26: To spell compound words; to join using a horizontal join.

Extra

Select words from each box that you can join to make new compound words.

finger
ginger
grass
hair
head
lady
life
lip
news
sauce

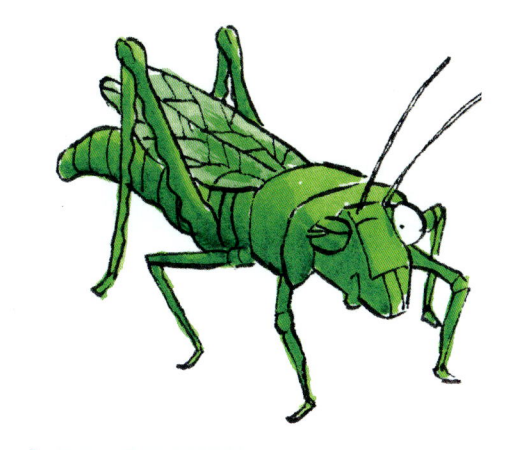

print
paper
stick
bird
bread
pan
guard
hopper
brush
ache

Extension

Some compound words have the same parts, for example, **tooth**paste, **tooth**brush and **tooth**pick. How many compound words can you make that contain the words below?

sun

ball

room

box

55

Yellow 27

Homophones

A b**are** b**ear**!

TIP Homophones sound the same but look different. You need to learn which spelling goes with which meaning!

Focus A

Copy these letter patterns into your book.

re re re re re re   are are are are are

ire ire ire ire ire ire   ore ore ore ore ore

Focus B

word bank
- sale / sail
- tale / tail
- bare / bear
- hare / hair
- pear / pair
- fare / fair
- more / moor
- pore / pour
- deer / dear
- here / hear
- tier / tear
- pier / peer
- tire / tyre
- there

Copy the correct spelling. Use your dictionary to help you.

1. pore / pour
2. bear / bare 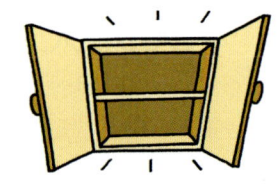
3. hair / hare 
4. tyre / tire 
5. deer / dear 
6. fare / fair 

56 Yellow 27: To spell homophones; to join the letters 'r' and 'e'.

Extra

Choose the correct homophone. Copy the sentences into your book.

1. There was only one [tyre] [tire] on the car.

2. The [bare] [bear] was taller than the tallest child.

3. The bus conductor collected my [fare] [fair] to the beach.

4. The dog chased the [hair] [hare] across the field.

5. I picked a [pair] [pear] from the tree in the orchard.

Extension

Some words have more than one homophone.
How many homophones can you write for each of these words?

- two
- there
- or
- paws
- rain
- by

Yellow 28

Irregular past tense

TIP Remember: **b, g, j, p, q, x, y** and **z** are break letters. They do not join to the letters that come after them.

I fr*oze* then I cr*ept* and I c*augh*t my *bro*ther.

Focus A

Copy the letter patterns into your book.

ept   ept ept ept ept   ugh   ugh ugh ugh ugh

bro   bro bro bro bro   oze   oze oze oze oze

Focus B

word bank

thought
brought
crept
swam
slept
built
caught
ran
flew
dealt
bit
shone
hung
froze
out

Pair present and past tenses of the same verb, for example, **sleep** and **slept**. Write them in your book.

sleep   built   swim

catch   creep   thought

build   think   slept

caught   swam   crept

TIP These words, in the past tense, have an unusual way of being spelled: for example, **sleep** becomes **slept** (not **sleeped**).

58 Yellow 28: To spell irregular past tenses; to form and write break letters.

Extra

Copy and complete these sentences by adding the past tense.

1. Today I bite my apple, yesterday I _____ it.

2. Today I deal the cards, yesterday I _____ them.

3. Today I freeze in the cold, yesterday I _____ in it.

4. Today I hang my picture, yesterday I _____ it.

5. Today the sun will shine, yesterday the sun _____.

Extension

Look at the pictures showing the things Lucia did yesterday. How many sentences can you write about her day?

Yellow 29 Irregular plurals

The m*ice* and the wol*ves* like showing their t*ee*th!

Focus A

Copy the letter patterns into your book.

ves ves ves ves ves   res res res res res

wes wes wes wes wes   oes oes oes oes oes

Focus B

TIP
If a word ends in **f**, change it to **v** and add **es**:
wolf → wolves.
Words with **oo** often change to **ee**:
tooth → teeth.
Words with **ous** often change to **ice**:
louse → lice.
Words with **a** often change to **e**:
man → men.

word bank
- children
- women
- men
- calves
- knives
- wolves
- mice
- lice
- geese
- feet
- teeth
- people

Write the single version of these plural words. Use your dictionary.

1. women
2. knives 
3. mice 
4. people 
5. geese 
6. calves 

60 Yellow 29: To spell irregular plurals; to join using a horizontal join.

Extra

Copy and complete these sentences by adding the plural.

1 One man, a few _____.

2 One calf, lots of _____.

3 One child, two _____.

4 One person, lots of _____.

5 One sheep, some _____.

Extension

Copy and complete these sentences using a collective noun.

1 A _____ of wolves.

2 A _____ of fish.

3 A _____ of puppies.

4 A _____ of bees.

5 A _____ of lions.

pride   shoal   swarm   pack   litter

Yellow 30

Review

Focus

Unscramble the sentences. Write them in your book.

1. sunny It today. is 
2. Tomorrow running. I will go
3. geese. I see can flock a of 
4. teacher My is great!
5. you to play? Can come out
6. think rain I it later. might
7. you do eat What want to tonight?

Yellow 30: To review sentence structure and spelling.

Extra

Write as many words as you can using all of the letters from each box. For example, using S T P, you can write **stop, step, tops, past, taps** and **pasta**.

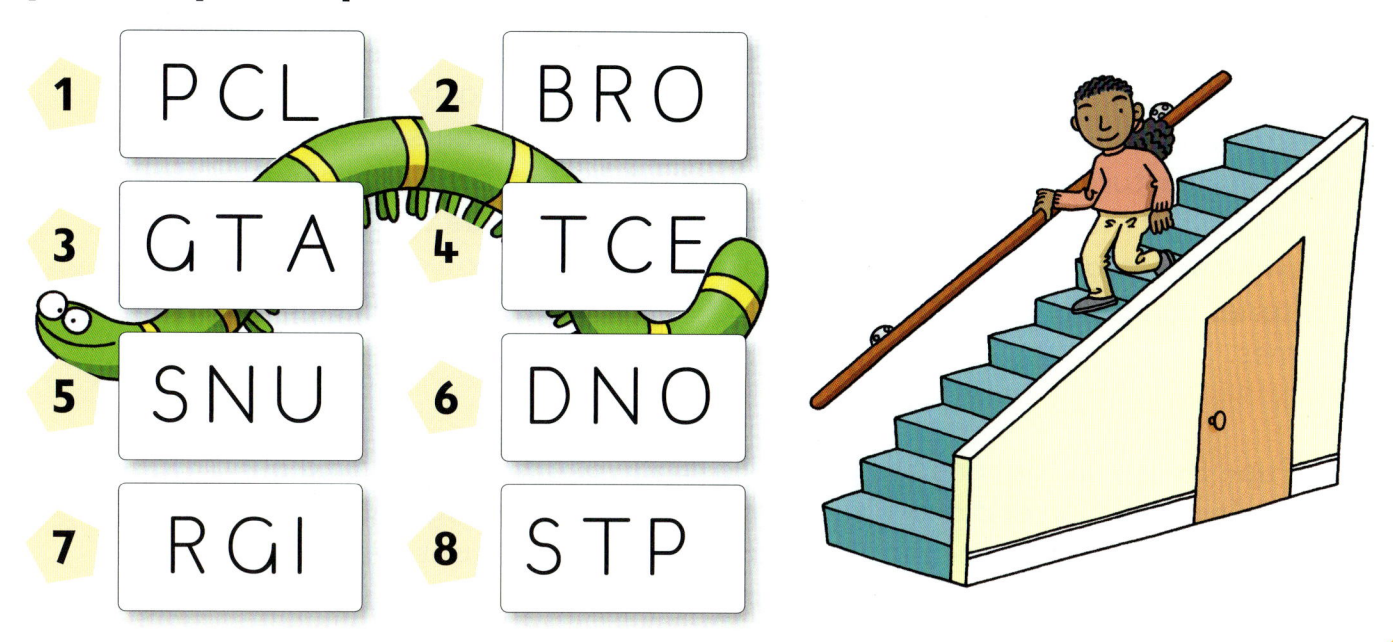

1. P C L
2. B R O
3. G T A
4. T C E
5. S N U
6. D N O
7. R G I
8. S T P

Extension

Write three sentences, each one containing two of these words. See how silly you can make them!

canaries

shark

humbug

jelly

pyjamas

sailing

anorak

tractor

Yellow 30: To review sentence structure and spelling.

How to use this book

The Yellow Pupil Book consists of 30 units that help to teach the key skills of spelling and handwriting alongside a systematic phonics course. Each unit is carefully structured to provide both full support for less able pupils and to extend the learning of more able pupils, and can be used alongside the *Nelson Phonic Spelling and Handwriting* Teacher's Book, Yellow Workbooks and the CD-ROM. This series can also be used alongside the *Nelson Spelling* and *Nelson Handwriting* schemes.

The Pupil Books are designed to provide a range of activities to build on whole-class teaching and group teaching of phonics, spelling and handwriting (provided through the Teacher's Book and CD-ROM). It uses simple logos to indicate the skill (or skills) each activity involves:

Phonic – this activity involves recognising, saying or hearing a phoneme or word.

Spelling – this activity involves spelling graphemes or words.

Handwriting – this activity involves handwriting letters, graphemes or words.

The Pupil Book activities are split into three levels:

Focus — These are phonic, spelling and handwriting activities which all children should be able to attempt with reasonable success.

Extra — These are phonic, spelling and handwriting activities which most children should be able to attempt.

Extension — These are phonic, spelling and handwriting activities which the most able in the class should be able to do.

All the units are illustrated in full colour in order to provide cues and engaging discussion points when tackling the phonic, spelling and handwriting activities.